CRISTIANO RONALDO

ODYSSEYS

MICHAEL E. GOODMAN

CREATIVE EDUCATION · CREATIVE PAPERBACKS

Published by Creative Education and Creative Paperbacks
P.O. Box 227, Mankato, Minnesota 56002
Creative Education and Creative Paperbacks are imprints of
The Creative Company
www.thecreativecompany.us

Design and production by Tom Morgan
Art direction by Blue Design

Images by Associated Press/Lalo R. Villar, 55; Corbis/ALBERT GEA/Reuters, 8, Antonio Cotrim/epa, 27, Jose Manuel Ribeiro/Reuters, 28, 40, RICH FATON/epa, 32; Dreamstime/David Ribeiro, 2, Dan Grytsku, 63, Fabio Diena, 36, Hris86, 66, MaxiSports, 6, Natursports, 43, 44, Ocusfocus, 39, Vladyslav Moskovenko, 4-5, 12-13, 16, 52, Zeytun Images, 56; Getty Images/ADRIAN DENNIS, 21, Al Nassr FC, cover, 60, 64, Europa Press Entertainment, 69, 70-71, Mohammed Saad/Anadolu, 75, Tony Marshall - EMPICS, 18; Unsplash/Mony Misheal, 22, Vishal Butolia, 59; Wikimedia Commons/Ank Kumar, 51, Francesco Prota, 11, https://www.flickr.com/people/gowestphoto/, CC BY 2.0, 48, Oleg Dubyna, 79

Every effort has been made to contact copyright holders for material reproduced in this book. Any omissions will be rectified in subsequent printings if notice is given to the publisher.

Copyright © 2026 Creative Education, Creative Paperbacks
International copyright reserved in all countries. No part of this book may be reproduced in any form without written permission from the publisher.

Library of Congress Cataloging-in-Publication Data
Names: Goodman, Michael E. author
Title: Cristiano Ronaldo / by Michael E. Goodman.
Description: Mankato, Minnesota : Creative Education and Creative Paperbacks, [2026] | Series: Odysseys in sports. Soccer stars | Includes bibliographical references and index. | Audience: Ages 12-15 | Audience: Grades 7-9 | Summary: "Cristiano Ronaldo has won five Ballon d'Ors and set the records for most Champions League and international competition goals. Relive the global icon's highs in this action-packed biography for early high school readers"– Provided by publisher.
Identifiers: LCCN 2025012507 (print) | LCCN 2025012508 (ebook) | ISBN 9798895811382 library binding | ISBN 9798896800910 paperback | ISBN 9798895812648 ebook
Subjects: LCSH: Ronaldo, Cristiano, 1985–Juvenile literature | Soccer players–Portugal–Biography–Juvenile literature | Champions League (Soccer tournament)–Juvenile literature
Classification: LCC GV942.7.R626 G6613 2026 (print) | LCC GV942.7.R626 (ebook) | DDC 796.334092 [B]–dc23/eng/20250531
LC record available at https://lccn.loc.gov/2025012507
LC ebook record available at https://lccn.loc.gov/2025012508

Printed in the United States

Cristiano Ronaldo is a living legend of world football (soccer).

CONTENTS

Introduction **9**

Wunderkind **17**

Wine and Whales 22

Learning Discipline, the Sporting Way 28

Premier League Champion **33**

Lucky Number 7 39

Pelé Predicts 43

Taking on Europe and the World **46**

The Golden Ball 51

Really High Jump 56

Exploring New Frontiers **61**

Museo CR7 63

A High-Priced Sports Car 70

Selected Bibliography **76**

Glossary **77**

Websites **79**

Index **80**

CRISTIANO RONALDO

Introduction

Early in 2019, both the Italian soccer team Juventus and the Spanish club Atlético Madrid qualified to play in the Champions League, a competition among the top football (soccer) clubs in Europe. In March, they faced off against each other in home-and-home matches. The team with the higher combined goal count would move forward in the competition. Atlético had won the first leg, 2–0,

OPPOSITE: Ronaldo helped his new club Juventus overcome a deficit and advance past Atlético Madrid in the Champions League in 2019.

in Madrid. So, to advance, Juventus would need to win the second match by at least three goals.

Thousands of rabid Italian football fans packed Juventus's home stadium in Torino. They were there to root for all the Juventus players, but their loudest cheers were directed toward the club's superstar forward, Cristiano Ronaldo from Portugal. Ronaldo was in his first season with Juventus, but he had previously won five **Ballon d'Or** trophies while a member of both Manchester United in England and Real Madrid in Spain. He was soon dominating the offense of his new club. Ronaldo's combination of speed, ball control, and ability to fire missiles into the net with either his right or left foot made him stand out. Plus, he was being paid a huge salary, and the fans wanted to make sure he was worth the money.

Juventus's home stadium in Torino

Ronaldo (7) celebrates with his team after the 2019 UEFA Nations League final.

As the contest with Atlético got underway, Ronaldo sped up and down the field from his left-wing position. In the 27th minute, he elevated his 6-foot-2 (187-centimeter) frame high above the other players crowded near the opponents' goal mouth and sent a powerful header beyond the goalkeeper's reach and into the net. It was the first goal that Atlético's keeper had given up in the team's last six matches. Soon after halftime, Ronaldo rushed into the goal area again and sent another header toward the net. As the ball crossed the goal line, the Italian television announcer shouted into his microphone, "CRISSSS-ti-a-a-a-a-a-NO!" The goal leveled the **aggregate** score at 2–2. And Ronaldo wasn't finished. With just four minutes left in regulation time, Juventus was awarded a **penalty kick**. Ronaldo calmly faced off against the goalkeeper, made a slight fake to get the goalie moving to his left, then blasted the ball into the opposite corner. Ronaldo had scored a **hat trick**, and Juventus moved ahead in the Champions League competition.

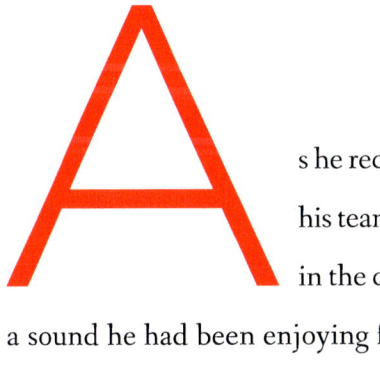

As he received excited hugs from his teammates, Ronaldo bathed in the cheers of the fans. It was a sound he had been enjoying for more than 16 years, since he played his first professional game in Portugal at age 17. He was sure that he had proven once again that he was the world's best "footballer."

CRISTIANO RONALDO

Wunderkind

On February 5, 1985, Cristiano Ronaldo was born in a poor neighborhood in Funchal, the capital of the island of Madeira. Madeira is in the Atlantic Ocean, 600 miles (966 kilometers) south and west of Portugal. People from Madeira speak Portuguese and are Portuguese citizens. The new baby was christened with the full name Cristiano Ronaldo dos Santos Aveiro. His mother chose Cristiano to connect him to his

OPPOSITE: Ronaldo lifts the UEFA Nations League trophy for Portugal in 2018-19.

Ronaldo in 2003

Catholic religion. His father added Ronaldo after his favorite actor Ronald Reagan, who was the U.S. president at the time. Cristiano's father, José Dinis Aveiro, worked as a gardener and was also the equipment manager at a local amateur soccer club. He asked the club's best player, Fernão Sousa, to be the baby's godfather.

One Christmas, when Cristiano was three or four, his godfather gave him a radio-controlled car to keep him busy. He broke into tears, saying what he really had wanted was his own football (soccer ball). He got one. "He slept with the ball," his godfather recalled, "and it never left his side. It was always under his arm. Wherever he went, it went with him."

"He could do amazing tricks with the ball," a childhood friend said. "It seemed to be stuck to his feet."

Cristiano's schoolteacher was not happy with his football obsession, however. "That ball is not going to feed you. You need school to reach your potential," she warned. But Cristiano was much happier and more successful playing ball than going to school. The places where he played in Funchal were rough—more like hilly rocky paths than open fields. He had to learn fancy footwork and careful **dribbling** to avoid holes and stones in the paths and good ball control to keep the soccer ball from rolling over the side of a hill. Those skills would indeed help to feed him as he moved forward in his soccer career.

At age eight, Cristiano's father brought him to the soccer club where he worked. Cristiano began playing with boys two to three years older than he was. Now, he could put those dribbling skills he had been practicing on the streets to work on a real soccer **pitch**. Some of his

A young Ronaldo leaps over an opponent.

Wine and Whales

Madeira, Cristiano's birthplace, is part of a group of four islands off the northwest coast of Africa. It is a very popular tourist destination. But even people who have never visited the islands still know the name because of their most famous product. Madeira wine, enjoyed all around the world, has been the islands' most important export since the 1600s. Tourists come to Madeira to drink wine and walk through lush gardens. They also board sightseeing boats and sail into the Atlantic Ocean to look for the many different types of whales that swim off the coast. These include spotted, striped, bottlenose, sperm, and beaked whales.

new football teammates called him "Crybaby" because he sometimes broke into tears when his teammates didn't pass to him or when he flubbed his passes to them. They also called him *abelhinha* ("little bee") because he buzzed non-stop around the field.

By the time Cristiano was 10 years old, people all around Madeira began hearing about the "wunderkind"—a German word meaning talented young child—who was showing off his skills at the small club. Nacional, a much larger club on the island, wanted to sign him up. Nacional offered the first club two sets of **kit** for each of its current players and 20 soccer balls as a **transfer fee**. A deal was made.

Cristiano's skills were so advanced that he outgrew playing for Nacional within two years. At the time, Nacional owed 25,000 euros (about $27,000) to Sporting for a transfer that had fallen apart. Sporting was a high-ranked professional team in Lisbon, the capital of Portugal. Nacional hoped Sporting would forgive the debt in return for signing Cristiano. Sporting flew Cristiano and his godfather to Lisbon for a tryout to see how good he was. It was his first plane trip.

The tryout went well. The report filed by the Sporting coaches described Cristiano as "two-footed, fearless, and daring." Soon, the wunderkind was living, playing, and going to school with 20 other boys in Lisbon. He moved into the Sporting club facilities, where he would remain until he turned 18. Most of the boys were 14 or older; Cristiano was the only 12-year-old. His mother, Maria Dolores, was very excited, however. Sporting was her favorite football team, and she already followed the club's games on television and radio.

Life at Sporting was difficult at first. The other boys made fun of Cristiano for his Madeiran accent. He had trouble making friends and felt very lonely. The little money he had went to pay for phone cards so he could call home. His mother convinced him to stick it out in Lisbon. "Football will put everything in its place," she predicted. And it did. At first, the other boys became annoyed at Cristiano for his tendency to dominate the ball on the pitch. Then they came to realize that it was better to give him the ball and let him lead them to victory.

Working out became Cristiano's new obsession. He would wake up in the middle of the night and sneak out of his dorm room to go to the gym. He would climb on the roof and then slip inside through an open window. Soon, the Sporting officials put locks on the windows to keep him out. "When I have a house, the first thing I'm going to build is my own gym," he told his new friends. He also began attaching weights to his ankles and running on the steep streets in Lisbon to build up his leg strength and speed.

Cristiano was assigned to the youth team (under-14) at Sporting, and soon players in the under-15 and under-16 groups were coming to watch his workouts and games. Everyone was impressed. Then, one day when he was 15, Cristiano felt a sharp pain in his chest. He had noticed that his heart often beat very quickly when he was playing, and he tired out easily. Doctors examined

Cristiano and his mother, Maria Dolores dos Santos Viveiros Aveiro

Learning Discipline, the Sporting Way

When Cristiano arrived at Sporting in Lisbon, he had a lot of raw talent but lacked self-control. He once threatened a teacher with a chair and talked back to a coach who had asked him to help clean the changing room. He received a wake-up call when he was not allowed to play in an important game against Marítimo, a club on Madeira. He had hoped to show off his skills on his home island. Cristiano was angry and hurt, but the coaches stood firm, and he did not travel to Madeira. The experience provided an important lesson to help Cristiano mature.

him and diagnosed that he had tachycardia, a dangerously high heart rate. They recommended laser surgery on his heart and got his parents' permission to operate. It took Cristiano three months to recover from the surgery before he was allowed to play again.

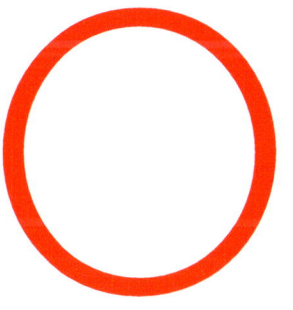nce back, Cristiano progressed amazingly quickly. During the 2001–02 season—before he turned 17—Cristiano was promoted several times. He went from Sporting's under-17 team, to the under-18 team, to the main club reserves, to the first team. Soon,

other European clubs began scouting the young wonder. Not all their first reports were encouraging. One scout reported: "The kid's technique is insufficient, and he lacks mental strength and concentration." Cristiano was annoyed to be called "kid," but he made sure to demonstrate both physical and mental strength on the pitch.

The following season, Cristiano received a new promotion. Sporting's first-team **striker** had transferred to a new team, so there was an opening. The team manager asked what the budget was to bring in a new striker and was told that the budget was zero. "Then, Cristiano will be our new striker," the manager said. Soon afterwards, the manager sent him off the bench into a tight 2–2 tie game with 15 minutes remaining. He took a pass near the opponent's goal. When the goalkeeper came out to meet him, Cristiano dribbled around him and lobbed the ball over two defenders into the net for the game winner.

Soon more scouts were in the stands during Sporting games to see Cristiano perform. He felt he was ready to move on to a better team. He hoped he would be transferred to a club in either Spain or England. "They're the best leagues in Europe," he said. In fact, he would play in both countries as his career progressed.

Premier League Champion

England would be Ronaldo's next stop on his journey to stardom. First, the British team Arsenal tried to work out a deal with Sporting, but the two sides couldn't come to terms. Ronaldo was disappointed, but he was eager to hear offers from other clubs. Soon British powerhouse Manchester United (called "United" or "ManU") decided

OPPOSITE: Ronaldo plays for Manchester United in 2009.

to make its own sales pitch. ManU had been scouting Ronaldo for several seasons. Its legendary manager Alex Ferguson read the scouting reports carefully and liked what he saw.

I n August 2003, ManU completed a playing tour in the United States and was heading back to England. On the way, the team stopped off in Lisbon to play a **friendly** against Sporting. Most of the ManU players were not looking forward to the match; they just wanted to get home. But the Sporting players and fans were thrilled. More than 50,000 fans turned out to see the game at Sporting's new stadium.

Cristiano got prepared for the match in his own unique way. He let his hair grow out long and added blonde streaks to his curls. He also wore a pair of flashy silver boots (soccer cleats). The ManU players noticed his appearance right away, but they took even more notice when they saw him play.

"He was doing **stepovers**, tricks, the whole thing, and the confidence he had was just unbelievable," recalled one United player. "He seemed to puff his chest out and was saying, 'This is my arena.'"

Cristiano led Sporting to a 3–1 victory in the friendly, and Alex Ferguson believed he had found a new star for his English club. After the match, the United team bus stayed near the Lisbon stadium for more than an hour.

Ronaldo plays for ManU in 2005.

The players wondered about the delay. Then they heard that Ferguson was trying to work out a deal for Cristiano. The players were all in favor of bringing him to England. The negotiations went quickly. Ferguson had been told that Arsenal had offered 8 million British pounds (about $10 million) and been rejected. "Then offer 9 million," said Ferguson. In the end, the transfer fee was settled at more than 12 million British pounds (about $15 million).

Cristiano made his debut at Old Trafford, ManU's stadium, on August 16, 2003, just 10 days after the friendly in Lisbon. He started out on the bench, wearing the number 7 jersey that former ManU star David Beckham had most recently worn. United got out to a 1–0 lead over Bolton; then the club's offense stalled. Midway through the second half, Ferguson sent Cristiano in as a substitute. He raced across the pitch, driving Bolton defenders crazy. He assisted on one goal and helped to set up another. The tempo of the game changed with Cristiano on the pitch, and United scored a 4–0 win.

"It looks like the fans have a new hero. It was a marvelous debut, almost unbelievable," said Ferguson. "I thought the pace was too slow in the first half, and I knew Cristiano would add penetration. We have to be careful with the boy. You must remember he is only 18. We are going to have to gauge when we use him."

Over the next few months, Cristiano had to make some major adjustments—to the style of English football,

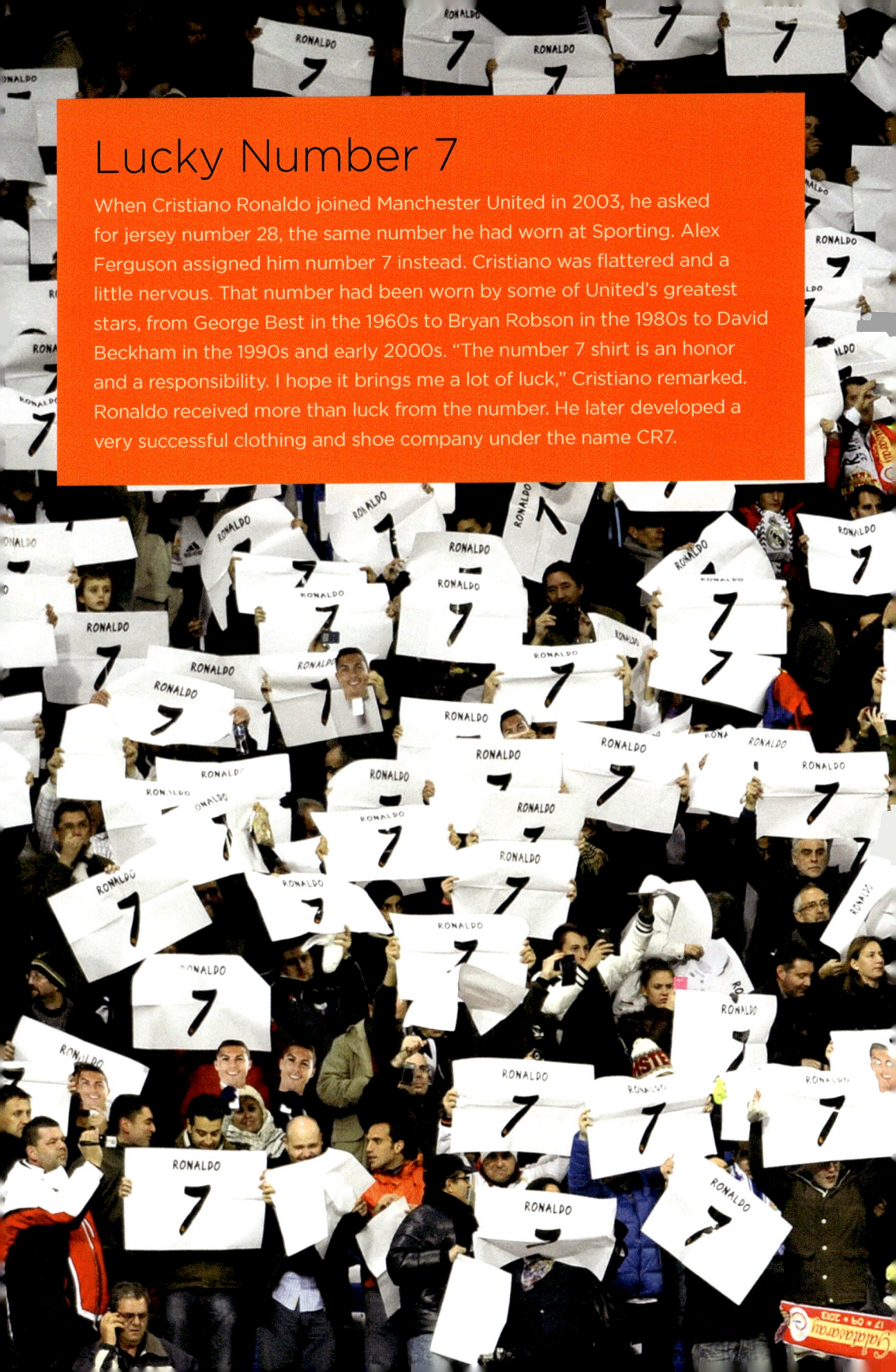

Lucky Number 7

When Cristiano Ronaldo joined Manchester United in 2003, he asked for jersey number 28, the same number he had worn at Sporting. Alex Ferguson assigned him number 7 instead. Cristiano was flattered and a little nervous. That number had been worn by some of United's greatest stars, from George Best in the 1960s to Bryan Robson in the 1980s to David Beckham in the 1990s and early 2000s. "The number 7 shirt is an honor and a responsibility. I hope it brings me a lot of luck," Cristiano remarked. Ronaldo received more than luck from the number. He later developed a very successful clothing and shoe company under the name CR7.

Ronaldo during training in 2004

to a different climate than he was used to, and to new foods and language. He soon moved into the starting lineup for United and helped power the team to a third-place finish in the English Premier League in 2003–04. At the end of the season, United fans voted him the winner of the club's Player of the Year award. He would earn the award three more times during his years with United.

Playing for United through the 2008–09 season, Cristiano became the driving force in the club's rise back to the top of English soccer. United won the Premier League title three years in a row between 2006 and 2009. The club also earned a Champions League title and won a FIFA Club World Cup competition.

For Cristiano, there were some major personal accomplishments too. During the 2007–08 season, he scored a remarkable 42 goals in 49 games for United and won the Golden Boot award as the top scorer in the Premier League. He tallied three of those goals during a 6–0 win over Newcastle United in January 2008. It was his first professional hat trick. (Through 2024, he had recorded 66 hat tricks, more than any other pro player.) Later in the year, the editors of *France Football* magazine voted him the 2008 Ballon d'Or winner by a wide margin. At the award ceremony in Paris, Cristiano was very emotional. "Winning the Ballon d'Or is something I have dreamt

Pelé Predicts

In January 2009, Cristiano received a special honor. He had been chosen for the first time as a finalist for the FIFA World Football Player of the Year award. At the awards ceremony, legendary soccer star Pelé of Brazil was asked to announce the winner. Pelé had been Cristiano's idol for a long time. Pelé began his presentation by saying, "Last year, I presented this trophy to Kaká (a Brazilian player for AC Milan in Italy). Afterwards, I shook Cristiano's hand and told him in Portuguese, 'Next year, I'll be giving it to you.'" Then Pelé opened the prize envelope, and, as he had predicted, the winner's name was "Cristiano Ronaldo."

Ronaldo plays for Real Madrid in 2011.

about since I was a little kid," he said with tears in his eyes. "I dedicate it to my family, who are here with me."

Winning his first Ballon d'Or seemed to be a perfect way for Cristiano to end his career in England. He had enjoyed his time with ManU, but Cristiano was starting to feel restless. He asked his agents to begin exploring opportunities in the Spanish La Liga, his other preferred location. Soon afterwards, representatives from Real Madrid, one of Spain's top teams, set up a meeting with Alex Ferguson and ManU business leaders. Negotiations went quickly, and on June 11, 2009, ManU agreed to accept Real's offer of 94 million euros (around $98 million). It was the highest transfer fee ever paid up to that time.

Taking on Europe and the World

Cristiano brought his high-scoring ways with him to Madrid. Just 35 minutes into his new club's first match of the 2009-10 La Liga season against Deportivo, he headed home a **corner kick** to put his side up 2-1 on the way to a 3-2 triumph. It was the first of a record 451 goals that Cristiano would tally for "Los Blancos" (the white shirts) in a total of 438 competitive matches. So, during his nine-season Real Madrid career (2009–2018), Cristiano scored, on average, more than a goal per game!

Real Madrid had long been one of the top clubs in Europe, but Cristiano's presence elevated the team to new levels. He helped Real win two La Liga titles, four Champions League crowns, three Club World Cups, three UEFA Super Cups, a pair of Copas del Rey, and two Spanish Super Cups. He also earned a trophy case full of individual honors. Those included four more Ballons d'Or, three Golden Boot awards, three UEFA Best Player in Europe trophies, and three Pichichi crowns as the top scorer in La Liga during a season.

Playing in La Liga also brought Cristiano into direct competition with the man who would become his biggest rival on the European and world stage—Lionel Messi of

2009 Real Madrid

Argentina, who played for Barcelona and later for Paris Saint-Germain. Those two men would dominate European soccer throughout the 2010s and into the 2020s. Messi's head-to-head record against Cristiano Ronaldo is 16 wins, 9 draws, and 11 defeats in competitive club matches. Messi also has one more goal to his name in their encounters, having scored 22 to Ronaldo's 21. But it is on the assist count that Messi really dominates with 11 goals created compared to just one from Ronaldo.

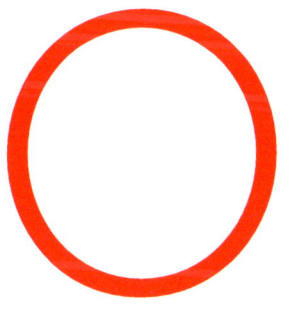One of Ronaldo's favorite encounters with Messi in Spain occurred in April 2012. Real Madrid had a slim lead over Barcelona in the La Liga standings, and a win by Real Madrid would probably guarantee them the title. With the game tied 1–1, Cristiano took a run toward the Barcelona goal. He controlled

a teammate's pass and shot from an almost impossible angle. The ball went in for the game winner. As the fans in Barcelona went a little crazy, Cristiano ran toward the stands and, with a hands-pushing-down motion, gestured for the fans to calm down. "Calma, calma, I'm here," he said in a soft but sarcastic way. Amazingly, his action silenced the crowd for a few seconds. That "calma" hand motion became a new way for Cristiano to celebrate goals he scored for Madrid, especially against Barcelona. He seemed to love upsetting opposing fans.

Ronaldo and Messi have also competed against each other on the world stage—during World Cup competitions, Champions League battles, and **Copa del Rey** encounters, for example. Representing Argentina and Portugal, respectively, Messi and Ronaldo have each played in five World Cups in their careers, with both participating

CRISTIANO RONALDO

2008

446 votos   **2** títulos   **42** goles   **49** partidos

The Golden Ball

The magazine *France Football* has been awarding a trophy to the top male football player in Europe every year since 1956. Most fans consider the Ballon d'Or to be soccer's highest individual honor. At first, the trophy was given only to athletes born in and playing in Europe. The requirements have since been expanded to enable professional footballers from clubs around the world to win. That expansion made Argentinian Lionel Messi eligible, and he received the trophy a record eight times between 2009 and 2023. Cristiano Ronaldo has won the ball five times, second most. The Ballon d'Or is not solid gold, but it is priceless to soccer fans.

2018 Champions League

in the 2006, 2010, 2014, 2018, and 2022 events. Messi has the edge in their World Cup competition because his Argentina squad won the 2022 Cup in Qatar, and he was named the most outstanding player of the tournament. Ronaldo did best Messi in one key way. In 2022, he became the first male player to score goals at five different World Cups. (Brazilian female footballer Marta—Marta Vieira da Silva—holds the same record for women.)

Ronaldo's scoring records in international competitions are unmatched by any other player. Wearing the green and red colors of Portugal in World Cup and UEFA competitions, he scored 135 international goals in 217 matches between 2002 and 2024. When, at age 33 and 130 days, he scored a hat trick in a 2018 World Cup match against Spain, he became the oldest player to accomplish that feat. In all, Ronaldo scored 10 hat tricks for Portugal in international matches.

Eventually, both Ronaldo and Messi moved on to teams outside of Spain. Messi went to Paris Saint-Germain in Ligue 1, the top level of French football. Ronaldo moved to Juventus in Serie A, the top Italian league. Real Madrid received a transfer fee of 100 million euros (about $105 million) to allow Ronaldo to leave and sign with Juventus. The signing was announced during the 2018 World Cup held in Russia. It became the top football story in the

Playing for Real Madrid in 2015

world that day, outshining news about France's victory over Belgium in the World Cup semifinals.

Ronaldo spent three seasons with Juventus, scoring 101 goals and leading the club to two Serie A titles. Then he decided to return to Manchester United. He explained the reasons he wanted to make the change.

Really High Jump

What do Michael Jordan and Cristiano Ronaldo have in common? Their ability to jump higher than their opponents to score. But Jordan had an advantage. He didn't have to use his head to send the ball into the net. The header was one of Cristiano's main weapons. He scored more than 150 goals on headers. Ronaldo's highest jump came during a match between his Real Madrid team and his former team Manchester United in the UEFA Champions League in 2013. Films show that he was 41.7 inches (1.06 meters) above the ground when he slammed the ball into the goal.

First, he had enjoyed his nine seasons in England and hoped to experience the same feeling as his career wound down. He also wanted to add at least two more Champions League titles to the record five wins he had already achieved in England and Spain. He felt ManU was the best club to help him accomplish that goal. On the day that Ronaldo's signing was announced, supplies of his number 7 ManU shirt flew off store shelves.

In the end, the move to ManU proved unsuccessful. Internal squabbles within United's management team and poor coaching decisions led Cristiano to give up on ManU after just 18 months. Plus, the aging superstar was slowing down on the pitch and didn't have the same breakaway speed he used to show. The two sides agreed to separate, and Cristiano announced that he was moving on to Al-Nassr in Saudi Arabia to open new football frontiers in the Middle East and Asia.

During his second stay with ManU, Ronaldo did accomplish one remarkable feat. In a game against Arsenal in December 2021, he converted a perfect pass from ManU teammate Marcus Rashford to record his 800th career goal in competitive matches. He was the first player to reach that mark. Since then, both Messi and Ronaldo have passed the 850-goal mark, and Ronaldo achieved number 900 during an international match between Portugal and Croatia in September 2024.

Portugal vs. Ghana, 2022 World Cup

CRISTIANO RONALDO

Exploring New Frontiers

The break with Manchester United officially came on December 30, 2022. During a press conference in Manchester, Cristiano said, "I did my mission in Europe well and achieved everything. Now it's time for a new challenge in Asia."

The announcement may have surprised some soccer fans, but Cristiano and his family had been preparing for the move to Saudi

OPPOSITE: Ronaldo left Europe in 2022 to play for Saudi club Al-Nassr.

61

Arabia for several months. The year 2022 had been a terrible one for the soccer star professionally and personally. On the professional side, Cristiano's difficulties blending successfully with his new teammates and coaches during his second tour in Manchester had been upsetting. The team had not achieved many of its goals, finishing sixth in the Premier League, far behind its crosstown rivals, Manchester City, who topped the league standings. Cristiano's goal scoring was down, and he sometimes looked sluggish on the pitch.

But the personal problems were more distressing. Cristiano and his longtime girlfriend, model Georgina Rodriguez, had been expecting twins in April. The new babies would join the four children the couple already shared. But the birth did not go well. The little girl, Bella Esmeralda, survived the birth, but her twin brother, who

Museo CR7

During his long football career, starting in Madeira and then on to mainland Portugal, England, Spain, Italy, and Saudi Arabia, Cristiano has been awarded more than 200 trophies and cups. Many were for team accomplishments, and others were individual honors. In 2013, he built a museum in Funchal to house his awards. The Museo CR7 was moved to a new, larger location in 2016. According to the museum's director, Cristiano's favorite exhibit is the European Cup that Portugal won in 2016 in a major upset over France. Also notable is a Real Madrid jersey printed with "Ronaldo 324 Histórico" on the front to mark his becoming the club's all-time top scorer.

Ronaldo in an Al-Nassr jersey

would have been named Angel, died. "This year, I had the best and the worst moment of my life in an instant," Rodriguez said. For Cristiano, who seldom shared much about his personal life in public, the baby's death was a painful shock. It offered another reason for him to want to leave England and go to Saudi Arabia.

Why had he chosen Saudi Arabia for his next professional move? Besides wanting to join a different league away from Europe, Cristiano liked what he had learned about

Riyadh Stadium

Saudi Arabia's efforts to build up its soccer programs. The country was improving and expanding current soccer stadiums and facilities and building new ones in anticipation of the 2034 World Cup it was set to host. The team Cristiano was joining, Al-Nassr, had won nine Saudi Pro Premier League titles and had done well in

"THE MOVE TO RIYADH WAS MORE THAN A SPORTS DECISION FOR CRISTIANO. 'I SEE FOOTBALL AS A BUSINESS.'"

recent Asian Football Confederation (AFC) Champions League tournaments. Fittingly, the name Al-Nassr means "victory" in Arabic.

The move to Riyadh was more than a sports decision for Cristiano. "I see football as a business," he told British journalist Piers Morgan during a television interview. The 2.5-year contract he signed was the richest in sports history up to that time—more than 200 million euros (approximately $210 million), of which 72.5 million euros (approximately $74.2 million) was for playing football and the remainder was to cover his roles as a business generator and ambassador for the club. He was sure that his own business interests and Saudi Arabia's football brand could benefit from the agreement. On Instagram, the club went from 860,000 followers to 23 million in one year. The added exposure had a very positive effect on Ronaldo's own CR7 fashion and lifestyle brand, which includes clothing, shoes, and hotels in Lisbon, Madeira, Madrid, Marrakesh, and New York. Cristiano was now the third-highest earning sports star in the world behind Messi and LeBron James.

Al-Nassr's leaders also saw bringing Cristiano on board as a great move for business and social life in Saudi

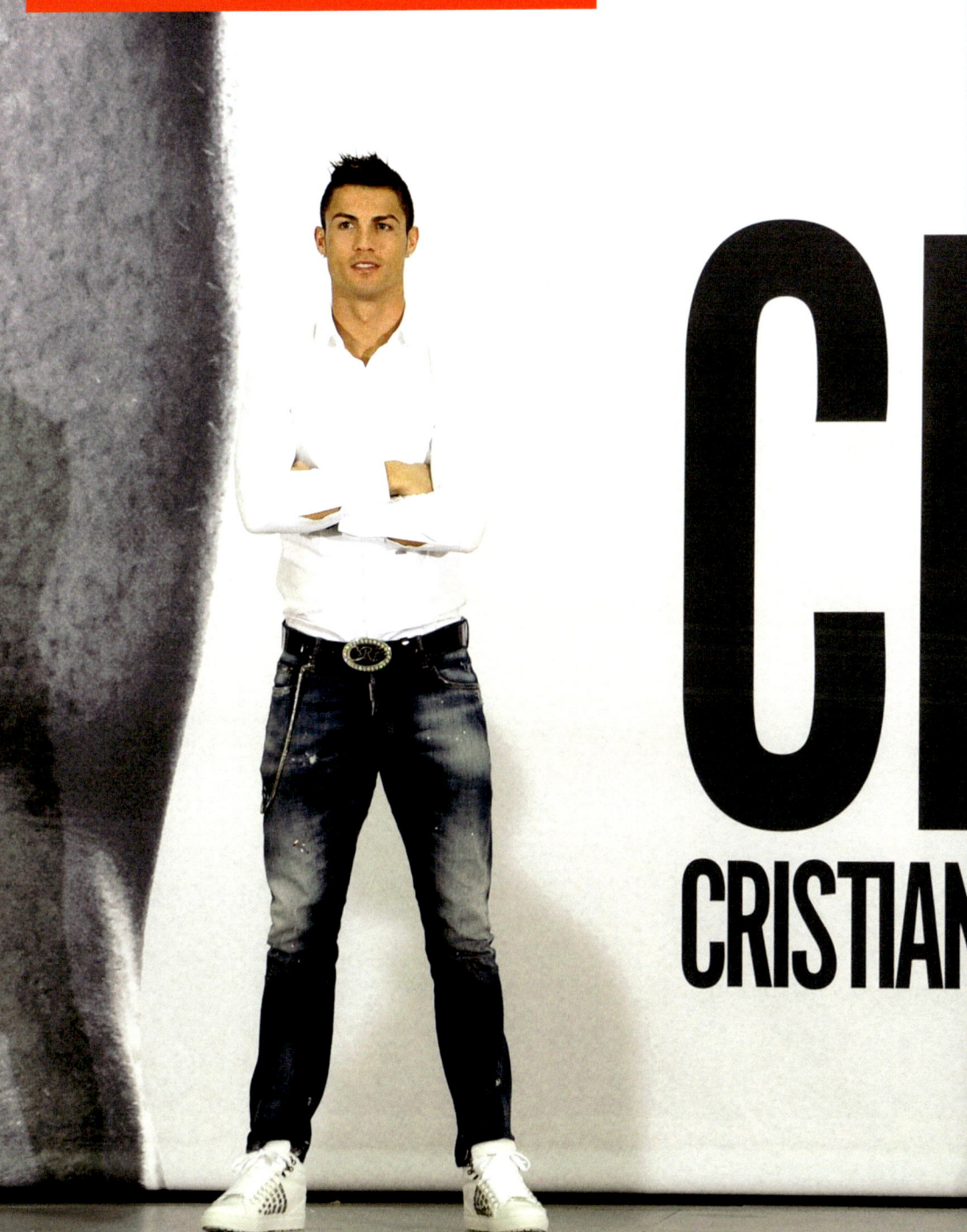
Ronaldo launches his CR7 underwear line in 2013 in Madrid.

A High-Priced Sports Car

According to a famous Italian chef, Cristiano Ronaldo treats his body like a high-priced sports car. He makes sure to give it the right fuel every day. The chef, Giorgio Barone, cooked for Cristiano many times when he played for Juventus in Italy. He learned that Cristiano doesn't enjoy luxury foods. Instead, he eats six small, healthy meals a day, so that he gets a boost of energy every three hours. "The best training doesn't help if it's not combined with a good diet," Cristiano says. "I eat a high-protein diet with lots of wholegrain products, eat fruit and vegetables, and avoid all sugary foods." His discipline is impressive!

Arabia now and in the future. "This is a signing that will not only inspire our club to achieve even greater success but inspire our league, our nation, and future generations of boys and girls to be the best version of themselves," the club announced on its social media platform.

Al-Nassr fans were excited to watch Cristiano perform on the pitch, but they were more concerned with how the team would do in league standings and tournaments. They got their answer quickly. In Cristiano's first season with the club, he won the league scoring title, and Al-Nassr achieved its highest league point total ever during the regular season. The team also won the Arab Club Champions Cup during the season for the first time. Cristiano had been the tourney star, scoring a **brace** in a 2–1 victory over rivals Al-Hilal in the final. After the match, he proudly held up the tournament trophy while fans cheered jubilantly.

Cristiano Ronaldo had come a long way from his humble beginnings on the Portuguese island of Madeira in the south Atlantic Ocean to his current lavish home in Saudi Arabia. He has enjoyed one of the most successful sports careers of any athlete in the world and has earned millions—paid to him in pounds, euros, and dollars, depending on where he was playing soccer. He also built a very successful business beyond sports. The soccer ball that his teacher on Madeira had predicted would never feed him has done just that. Very few other footballers in history have performed on the pitch with the same combination of speed, power, and trickery as Cristiano.

How long does he plan to keep playing, having now passed his 40th birthday? Cristiano was asked that question in his Piers Morgan interview when he left Manchester United. He tried to answer as honestly as he could. "The moment I feel I'm done, I'll retire . . . so maybe in ten years!"

Al-Hilal vs. Al-Nassr in 2025

Selected Bibliography

Balagué, Guillem. *Cristiano Ronaldo: The Award-Winning Biography.* London: Orion Publishing Group. Kindle Edition, 2024.

Caioli, Luca. *Ronaldo.* London: Corinthian Books, 2012. Updated 2018.

Dempsey, Luke. *Club Soccer 101: The Essential Guide to the Stars, Stats, and Stories of 101 of the Greatest Teams in the World.* New York: W.W. Norton & Company, 2014.

Goldblatt, David, and Johnny Acton. *The Soccer Book: The Sport, the Teams, the Tactics, the Cups.* 3rd ed. New York: DK, 2014.

Marshall, Ian. *Old Trafford: The Official Story of the Home of Manchester United.* London: Simon & Schuster, 2010.

Robinson, Joshua and Jonathan Clegg. *Messi vs. Ronaldo: One Rivalry, Two Goats.* New York: HarperCollins Publishers, 2022.

Glossary

aggregate — the combined number of goals scored by two teams over two or more games

Ballon d'Or — an award presented to the world's best player

brace — a pair of goals scored by one player in the same game

Copa del Rey — annual competition of Spanish teams

corner kick — a kick awarded to the offensive team when the whole of the ball passes over the goal line, either on the ground or in the air, having last touched a defending player, and a goal is not scored

dribbling — the skill of moving a soccer ball around the field using your feet while keeping control of it, without assistance from other players

FIFA — stands for Fédération Internationale de Football Association (French), the governing body for soccer national teams and clubs around the world

friendly — a contest played between two teams that doesn't count in any league standings

hat trick — three goals scored by one player in the same game

kit	the whole uniform a soccer team wears from the jersey to the shorts down to the socks
penalty kick	a direct kick is awarded to the attacking team when a defender inside his own penalty area commits a major foul. The kick is taken from the penalty spot. Only the kicker and the goalkeeper are allowed in the penalty area.
pitch	a soccer field
stepover	a dribbling move in soccer that involves stepping over the ball, faking a pass, and then quickly moving in the opposite direction
striker	a forward on a soccer team whose job is primarily to shoot and score
transfer fee	the price a buying club offers a selling club when a player moves, or transfers, from one club to another
UEFA	stands for Union of European Football Associations, the governing body for European national teams and clubs

Websites and videos

Cristiano Ronaldo
https://www.cristianoronaldo.com/#cr7
Cristiano Ronaldo's official website, with information on Cristiano's career highlights and achievements. There is also a link to sign up for the athlete's newsletter.

Cristiano Ronaldo
https://www.realmadrid.com/en-US/the-club/history/football-legends/cristiano-ronaldo-dos-santos-aveiro
A page dedicated to Cristiano on Real Madrid's website

https://www.youtube.com/watch?v=tU16fvTaK3U
A video in which Ronaldo demonstrates his remarkable ability to control a soccer ball during games

Index

Al-Hilal, 73, 75
Al-Nassr, 57–58, 61, 66–67, 68, 73, 75
Arab Club Champions Cup, 73
Arsenal, 33, 37, 58
Atlético Madrid, 9, 14
Ballon d'Or, 10, 11, 42, 45, 51
Barcelona, 48, 49, 50
Barone, Georgio, 70
Beckham, David, 37, 39
CR7, 39, 63, 68
Ferguson, Alex, 34, 35, 37, 39, 45
FIFA Club World Cup, 42, 47
FIFA World Cup, 50, 53, 54, 55, 59, 66
France Football magazine, 42, 51
Funchal, Madeira, 17, 20, 63
hat trick, 15, 43, 52, 54
Jordan, Michael, 56
Juventus, 9, 10, 14, 15, 54, 55, 70
La Liga, 45, 46, 47, 49
Lisbon, Portugal, 24, 25, 26, 28, 34, 35, 37, 68
Madeira, 17, 23, 25, 28, 63, 68, 73
Manchester City, 62
Manchester United (ManU), 10, 21, 33, 34, 35, 36, 37, 39, 45, 55, 56, 57, 58, 61, 74
Marta (Marta Vieira da Silva), 53
Messi, Lionel, 47, 48, 49, 50, 53, 54, 58, 68
Morgan, Piers, 67, 74
Museo CR7, 63
Nacional, 23, 24
Old Trafford, 37
Paris Saint-Germain, 48, 54
Pelé, 43
Pichichi crown, 47
Portugal national football team, 50, 53, 54, 58, 59, 63
Premier League, 41, 42, 62, 66
Rashford, Marcus, 58
Real Madrid, 10, 45, 47, 48, 49, 54, 56, 63
Riyadh, Saudi Arabia, 66, 67
Rodriguez, Georgina, 62, 65
Serie A, 54, 55
Sporting, 24, 25, 26, 28, 29, 30, 31, 33, 34, 35, 39
tachycardia, 29
UEFA Champions League, 9, 15, 36, 42, 47, 50, 52, 56, 57, 67
UEFA Nations League, 12, 17